STEP-UP

HISTORY

Children in Victorian Times

Jill Barber

First published in this edition in 2011 by
Evans Brothers Limited
2A Portman Mansions
Chiltern Street
London W1U 6NR

Produced for Evans Brothers Limited by
White-Thomson Publishing Ltd,
2 St. Andrew's Place,
Lewes, East Sussex, BN7 1UP

Printed by New Era Printing Company Limited in
Chai Wan, Hong Kong, March 2011, Job Number
CAG1628

Project manager: Ruth Nason

Designer: Helen Nelson, Jet the Dog

Consultant: Rosie Turner-Bisset, Reader in
Education and Director of Learning and
Teaching, Faculty of Education, University of
Middlesex.

British Library Cataloguing in Publication Data

Barber, Jill

Children in Victorian times - (Step-up history)
1. Children - Great Britain - History - 19th
century - Juvenile literature
2. Children - Great Britain - Social conditions
- 19th century - Juvenile literature
3. Great Britain - History - Victoria 1837-1901
- Juvenile literature
literature
I. Title
305.2'3'0941'09034

ISBN: 9780237543815

Picture acknowledgements:

Every effort has been made to trace copyright
holders. If any have been omitted from the
following list, the Publishers will correct this
at reprint.

Bridgeman Art Library: page 8 (© Harris Museum
and Art Gallery, Preston, Lancashire); City of
Westminster Archives Centre: cover (main) and
pages 17t, 24t, 25; Mary Evans Picture Library:
pages 4, 5b, 6t, 9, 11c, 12t, 13t, 13b, 16;
Hertfordshire Archives and Local Studies: pages 23,
26t; Hitchin Museum: page 19; Luton Museum:
pages 1 and 27; Manchester Library and
Information Service: Manchester Archives & Local
Studies: page 11t; W. D. Neal: page 15; Salvation
Army: page 26b; Shaftesbury Society: page 17b;
The National Archives: pages 5t, 20; Topfoto: cover
(top left) and pages 11b, 12b. The photos on the
cover (top right) and pages 6b, 7t, 7c, 7b are from
the author's collection.

Thanks also to Gloucestershire Record Office for
the Vicar's letter and logbook entry, page 25.

Contents

Queen Victoria

Queen Victoria was 18 when she became queen in 1837. When she was 21 she married her cousin, Prince Albert, who came from Germany. She proposed to him, because she was the queen. They had nine children, whom they loved very much.

Victoria was lonely as a child, so she enjoyed spending time with her children. Prince Albert was a strict father who believed that children should work hard, but he also enjoyed playing games with his children. Their happy family life became a model for all Victorian families.

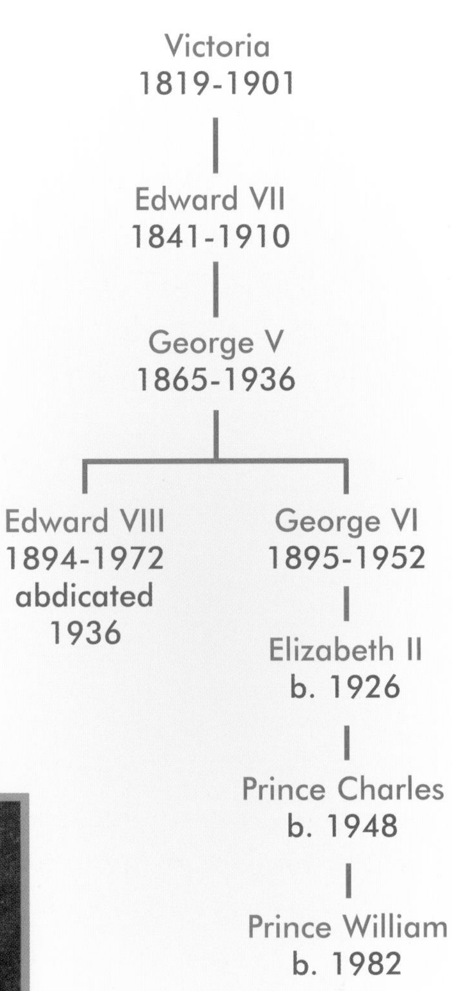

▲ *See if you can explain how the present queen, Elizabeth II, is related to Queen Victoria.*

◀ *This picture of Queen Victoria's family was painted in the summer of 1846. How has the artist tried to show that they are a happy family?*

Finding out about the Victorians

The people who lived during Queen Victoria's reign (1837-1901) are called Victorians. We can find out about their lives from photographs, diaries, letters, newspapers and reports created at the time.

One useful source is the census. See if you can use the census return below, to find out the names of the children in the painting on page 4. Who is shown as the 'head' of the family? In Victorian times, the man was always in charge.

Parish ~~or Township~~ of St. George Hanover Square		~~Ecclesiastical District of~~		City ~~or Borough~~ of Westminster			~~Town of~~
No. of Householder's Schedule	Name of Street, Place, or Road, and Name or No. of House	Name and Surname of each Person who abode in the house, on the Night of the 30th March, 1851	Relation to Head of Family	Condition	Age of Males	Age of Females	Rank, Profession, or Occupation
1	Buckingham Palace	Her Majesty Alexandrina Victoria	Wife	Mar		31	The Queen
		H.R.H. Francis Albert Augustus Charles Emanuel	Head	Mar	31		Duke of Saxony Prince of Coburg and Gotha
		H.R.H. Victoria Adelaide Mary Louisa	Daur			10	Princess Royal
		H.R.H. Albert Edward	Son		9		Prince of Wales
		H.R.H. Alice Maud Mary	Daur			7	Princess
		H.R.H. Alfred Ernest Albert	Son		6		Prince of the United Kingdom Duke of Saxony Prince of Coburg and Gotha
		H.R.H. Helena Augusta Victoria	Daur			4	Princess
		H.R.H. Louisa Carolina Alberta	Do			2	Princess
		H.R.H. Arthur William Patrick Albert	Son		11m		Prince of the United Kingdom Duke of Saxony Prince of Coburg and Gotha

This is the 1851 census return for Buckingham Palace. It shows that Queen Victoria's first name was Alexandrina. Her eldest son was known as Bertie. When he became king, he was called King Edward. Can you see why?

This photograph shows Queen Victoria with her son Edward, grandson George, and great-grandson Edward. Find them on the timeline on page 4.

Prince Albert

In 1861 Prince Albert died of typhoid and Queen Victoria was devastated. For the rest of her life she wore black in mourning.

She was 81 when she died in 1901. Her reign lasted for 64 years, longer than any other British king or queen.

Family fun

Life was very different for children in rich and poor families. Like the royal family, many Victorian families began to spend more time together. Musical evenings were popular and rich (upper-class) families went to concerts and the theatre. Middle-class families made their own entertainment, such as singing around the piano at home. Poor (working-class) families worked long hours and often found their entertainment in the street. In 1842, William Laws, aged 10, a poor boy from Durham, said: 'I play at marbles; throw a ball at the wall; play at running and catch another boy; play at the hoop; quarrel with other boys.'

A mechanical organ, pulled by a horse, is playing in the street. Are the dancing children rich or poor? A popular Victorian toy was a metal hoop, bowled along with a stick. Can you see one?

Holidays

In early Victorian times holidays were only for the rich. After 1871, when bank holidays were introduced, many working-class families began to have a day's outing to the seaside.

William and Jane Smith and their nine children went on a day trip to Cleethorpes in 1877. They all have hats. It was not respectable to be without one.

Photography

Photography was invented in Victorian times. In the 1850s, after Queen Victoria and Prince Albert were photographed, everyone wanted pictures of themselves and their children.

Having your photograph taken was a special occasion, so children wore their best clothes. They had to stay still for 40 seconds while the picture was taken, as cameras were not 'instant' as they are today. Can you be still and smile for that long?

▲ *What toy is this boy holding? He is wearing a dress, which was quite usual for boys until they were five.*

▼ *Winnie's brothers, Walter and Edgar, are wearing sailor suits. These became popular after Queen Victoria's eldest son wore one.*

▲ *Children's clothes were not designed for play. This girl is wearing a smaller version of adult clothes.*

Become a photographer

Try taking a photograph of someone in your family, or a friend, with their favourite toy. Compare your photograph with those on this page. What changes do you notice?

Life on the land

At the beginning of the nineteenth century, 70 per cent of people lived in rural areas, where life could be very hard for poor children. Farm labourers' wages were low and children started work young so that their families could afford enough food.

The youngest children were employed in the fields as bird scarers, to stop birds eating the crops. The work was not hard, but could be very lonely. From the age of 8, boys became ploughboys, leading the horses. Girls did back-breaking jobs such as stone picking and weeding, but were often needed at home to look after the younger children.

Small children had to frighten the birds away from crops by making a loud noise with a wooden rattle. 'Bird Scaring, March' was painted by Sir George Clausen in 1896.

Enquiring into working conditions

In 1867 Parliament set up a Commission of Enquiry into children's working conditions in agriculture. The Commissioners interviewed children around the country.

Alfred James, aged 13, from Dinham described his life to the Commissioners.

Began to work at 8, driving plough. Horses knocked me down once, but found I could manage them. Pays 3d a day … Up to 11 years of age came to school a few months and worked a few. Liked coming to school best. Made a boy terrible tired walking about with the horses.

▶ *This evidence was given by 16-year-old Thomas Hole from Bishops Lydeard. How many hours a day did he work?*

First went out to work at 8. Went to regular work at 9, when began to lead horses. Horses used to knock me down sometimes, but never hurt me; trod on my feet now and then. First work was keeping birds, Sundays as well as week days. Hours 5.30am to 7pm in barley sowing; wheat sowing 6.30am to 4.30pm because the days are shorter. None in August. Was paid 4d a day bird-keeping, and the same for ever so long after began regular work. Only had a dinner given me on Christmas Day. When I came home after being out in the rain had to dry myself as I best could at the fire; but often when it rained rigged up a hurdle with thatch to shelter me in the corner of a field. Never went to school at all.

▲ *Young boys in charge of horses were often not strong enough to control them. Many were badly injured or even killed by being crushed against carts or gateposts.*

Personal memories

When he was 80, Ralph Miles was asked for his personal reminiscence of life as a child at the beginning of Queen Victoria's reign. Agricultural labourers often had large families, and Ralph was one of a family of 14. How do you think this source might be affected by the time that has passed between the events and Ralph's memory of them?

'It was cruelly hard, we not only had to eat swedes, but we used to cook the rinds of the swedes for food … As for boots … my mother used to beg for them, and whatever the sizes were, we had to use them; if too small, our toes had to come outside … It was often cold, and when the boots were too big it was almost worse; our feet got so sore working in the fields.'
(Ralph Miles)

Oral history

Ask an older person you know to tell you about life when they were a child. Think about the questions you will ask. Tape-record the interview and make a note of the date and who is speaking. This is called oral history.

Factories

Families started to move from the land in search of work and a better life. By 1900 about 70 per cent of people were living in towns. Many found work in factories, but conditions were often very bad.

Factories and textile mills were keen to employ children because they could pay them less. Children's size was also an advantage as small bodies could squeeze underneath the machines to clean them. Small fingers were useful for tying broken cotton threads or changing lace bobbins.

Commission of Enquiry

Concern about children led to a Commission of Enquiry in 1832. Inspectors visited factories around the country. Here are three extracts from the evidence they collected for their Report.

Charles Aberdeen: 'The smallest children in the factories were scavengers … they go under the machine, while it is going … it is very dangerous when they first come, but they become used to it.'

Hannah Brown: 'I began work at the mill in Bradford when I was 9 years old … we began at 6 in the morning and worked until 9 at night. When business was brisk, we began at 5 and worked until 10 in the evening.'

▲ ***How many hours a day did Hannah work? Children were not allowed to sit down, and standing for hours caused their legs to become deformed.***

▼ ***What was William Rastrick's job? How do you think he made the children work? Do you think he was a bad man?***

William Rastrick: 'I work at the silk mill. I am an overlooker and I have to superintend the children at the mill. Their strength goes towards the evening and they get tired. I have been compelled to urge them to work when I knew they could not bear it. I have been disgusted with myself. I felt degraded and reduced to the level of a slave driver.'

◀ ***Can you see a scavenger in any of the pictures on page 11? What do you think was the danger of their work?***

The Enquiry found that serious injuries were common, especially when children were tired. For example, when one boy tried to clear some cotton out of a spinning machine, one of the wheels caught his finger and tore it off.

Evidence from pictures

Pictures can show us what the past was like, but how accurate are they? Pictures can be used as propaganda. Which of the pictures here, drawn in the 1830s and 1840s, do you think was used to:

- campaign for better working conditions for children in factories;
- show other countries that England had a successful cotton industry;
- illustrate a story about a poor factory boy?

Media check

Pictures are used in the media today to put across a particular message. Look at today's newspaper and see if you can find an example.

Mines

In 1842 Parliament made an enquiry into the lives of children who worked in coalmines. Many children were asked about their work. In the report of the enquiry you can read what the children said in their own words. The report also includes drawings like the four shown here.

Sarah Gooder, aged 8

'I'm a trapper in the Gawber pit. It does not tire me, but I have to trap without a light and I'm scared. I go at four and sometimes half past three in the morning, and come out at five and half past. I never go to sleep. Sometimes I sing when I've light, but not in the dark; I dare not sing then. I don't like being in the pit.'

Children as young as 4 or 5 were used as trappers. They had to sit in the dark, opening the doors for the coal trucks. If they fell asleep they could be crushed by the doors. Sometimes rats ate the bread and cheese that the children took for their dinner. Why was Sarah Gooder scared?

Older girls, such as Fanny Drake, worked as hurriers, pulling wagons of coal along a narrow tunnel.

Fanny Drake, aged 15

'I have been 6 years last September in a pit. I hurry by myself. I find it middling hard. It has been a very wet pit before the engine was put up. I have had to hurry up to my calves of my legs in water. I go down at 6 a.m. and sometimes 7; and I come out at 5, and sometimes 6. I don't like it so well. It's cold, and there's no fire in the pit … I push with my head sometimes, it makes my head sore sometimes, so that I cannot bear it touched; it is soft too. I have often had headaches, and colds, and coughs, and sore throats. I cannot read. I can say my letters.'

Accidents

To get up and down the narrow mine shaft, children had to cling on to a rope. Accidents were common. Tired children often fell off the rope, and sometimes the rope broke. Worst of all, children could be wound over the roller and crushed to death. David Pellett 'was drawn over the roller by his own uncle and grandfather … just at the moment when their attention was called to a passing funeral.'

Children under 13 killed in accidents in coalmines, 1838

Cause of death	Number of children
Fell down the shafts	13
Fell down the shaft from the rope breaking	1
Drawn over the pulley	3
Fall of stone out of a skip down the shaft	1
Drowned in the mines	3
Fall of stones, coal and rubbish in the mines	14
Injuries in coal pits	6
Explosion of gas	13
By tram wagons	4

In the mine shaft.

Which of the accidents recorded in 1838 is about to happen here?

Child labour today

Around the world today over 240 million children still work for low wages and in dangerous conditions, including in mines. Visit www.therightsite.org.uk to find out about children who are exploited and oppressed.

Chimney-sweeps

Coal fires were lit for warmth and cooking in Victorian homes, and chimneys became full of soot. Many chimneys were narrow and winding and the only way to clean them was to send small children up inside with a brush.

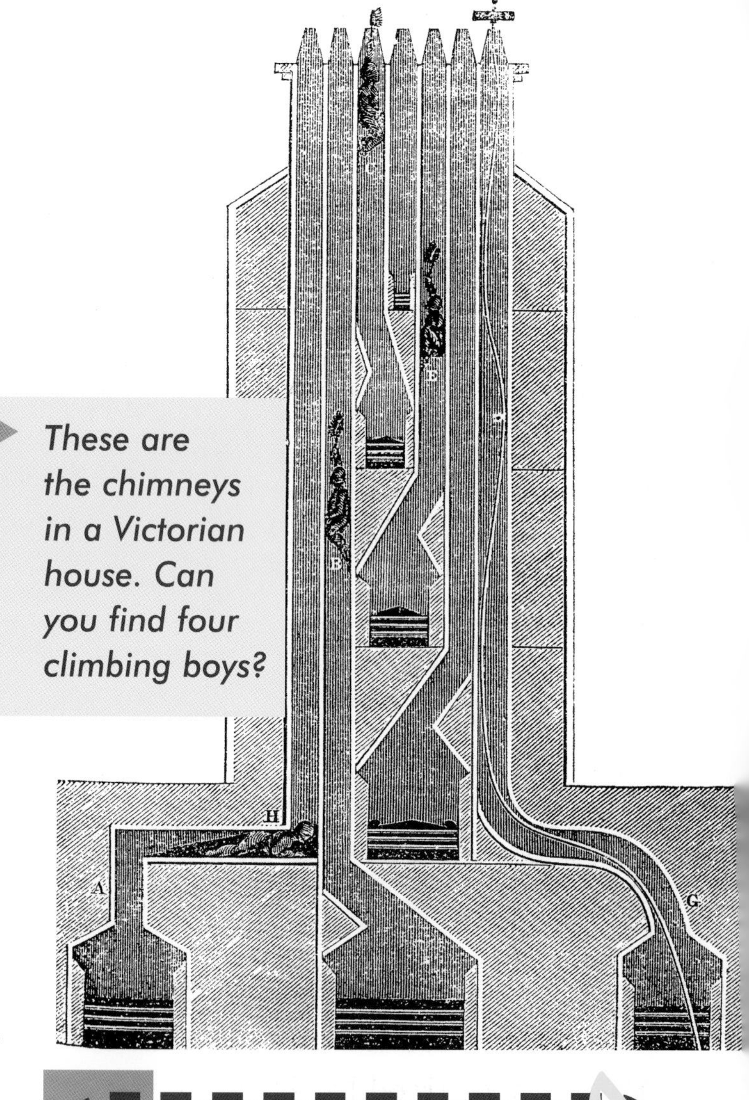

These are the chimneys in a Victorian house. Can you find four climbing boys?

Climbing boys

If you were a climbing boy (or girl) you had to work your way to the top by pressing your knees and elbows against the walls. As well as damage to arms and legs, you had to cope with soot falling on your face and filling your lungs.

Boys climbed with no clothes on because the chimneys were so narrow that they could get stuck. Very young children were used, and often half starved to keep them small. If a child did get stuck in a chimney, the sweep would light a fire underneath to make them struggle harder.

Tragic death of a climbing boy

In 1844 James Dye, aged 10, was suffocated to death in a chimney. Read the story on page 15. It was told many years later by Daniel Dye, the son of James's brother. Then compare the story with the newspaper report from the day after the inquest into James's death. How many differences can you find? Can you explain why there are differences? Who do you think was there at the time?

Would you fit?

Cut a hole 23 cm square in the centre of a sheet of card or newspaper. Now try to get through it. This is the size of some chimneys that children had to crawl through.

THE STORY TOLD BY DANIEL DYE

About 100 years ago my grandmother set off at 3 o'clock one morning with her donkey and 7 year old son [James] to sweep the chimneys at Goldings, then occupied by Sir Minto Farquhar, MP for Hertford. She arrived at Goldings at about 3.30 am, and having fixed the soot sheet round the kitchen chimney, put James into the flue and went outside to wait for his call from the chimney pot, which would prove to her that he had reached the top. She had just got back to the kitchen when she heard a noise near the fireplace. He must have slipped and fallen. She could hear him groaning, but could not get to him, and forbearing to waken the aristocratic household at such an hour, she set off at a run through the winter darkness towards Hertford to summon help. Attempting a short cut through the grounds she fell into the river and arrived wet through and exhausted. Builders' men were sought, the household aroused, and some hours later the brickwork at the chimney base was cut away and the body of the child recovered. He had fallen into a pocket of soot several feet deep and had been suffocated.

Sir Minto Farquhar was very upset, and he vowed that day to support the legislation against the use of climbing boys.

HERTFORD MERCURY

6 July 1844

On Friday (yesterday) evening, an inquest was held at Goldings, the seat of Lord Reay, on view of the body of a little boy named James Dye, who was suffocated in a shaft connected with the flues belonging to his lordship's kitchen. It appeared from the evidence that about 2 o'clock on Friday morning, James Dye, the father of the deceased, went to Lord Reay's for the purpose of sweeping the kitchen and scullery chimneys. Dye, contrary to the express orders of Lord Reay, took his little boy with him, and, finding it difficult to sweep soot from a ledge of the scullery flue, sent the boy up to throw it down.

The boy had been up the flue about a quarter of an hour, when he cried that he could not get down. The father told him to go up to the top, saying that, if he did so, he would go up the kitchen chimney and lift him out. The deceased, however, could not go up, and began moaning in a most dreadful manner. The father then obtained the assistance of some of the servants, and at 3 o'clock, Mr Mumford, a bricklayer, was sent for, and arrived about 4. It was, however, near 8 o'clock before the body of the boy could be extricated.

Who was to blame?

Was James Dye's father guilty of murder? The coroner decided it was an 'accidental death'. However he fined Mr Dye £10 (about £5,000 today) because, in 1840, an Act of Parliament had made it illegal to send children up chimneys. Many people ignored the law because they believed that boys cleaned chimneys better than machines. Others campaigned for better laws to protect children.

This photograph shows that Daniel and William Dye, the grandsons of Mr Dye, were working for the family business in 1895.

Lord Shaftesbury

One person who wanted to protect children was Lord Shaftesbury (1801-85). He had an unhappy childhood, although he was born into a rich family. His parents showed him no love and he was sent away to school, where he was badly treated.

In 1832 Lord Shaftesbury read a report in the *Times* about children in factories. It made him determined to help them. As an MP, he could speak in Parliament and try to get new laws to give children shorter working hours, better working conditions and access to education.

Here is Lord Shaftesbury visiting a coalmine in 1842. He wanted to see for himself how children had to work.

Changing the law

In 1833 a law called the Factory Act tried to limit the hours that children worked, but there were not enough inspectors to make sure that factory owners were keeping the law. A new law was passed in 1847 after Lord Shaftesbury campaigned for a 'Ten Hour Day'.

In 1840 he set up the Children's Employment Commission, which published its report on mines in 1842. Until then, most people had no idea that children worked in coalmines. This led to the Mines Act, which stopped children working underground.

▲ *Lord Shaftesbury visiting a Ragged School in Old Pye Street, Westminster, London, in 1846.*

Web search

Find out about other people who helped to make life better for children. What was the Children's Charter? Who was the first patron of the NSPCC? To find out, go to the 'What we do' section at www.nspcc.org.uk.

Ragged Schools

Many children's lives were changed because they had the chance to go to a Ragged School. After 1844, Lord Shaftesbury helped to set up more than 200 of these schools, which were for the poorest children. As well as reading and writing, girls were taught how to sew and boys learnt a skill such as shoemaking. Many of the schools met in the evenings because children had to work during the day.

▶ *Lord Shaftesbury inspired other people to help him. One of these was Adeline Cooper. She set up the One Tun Ragged School in Westminster, in 1853, in a pub that had been a den of thieves.*

Life in the workhouse

People who were desperate for food and shelter and too ill or weak to work could be taken into a workhouse. This was a feared and hated place, where life was made as unpleasant as possible. Parents were separated from their children, and food was little more than watery porridge called gruel.

Charles Dickens

Charles Dickens (1812-70) was a popular novelist, who used stories to make people realise what terrible conditions many poor people had to live in. As a child he was forced to work in a blacking factory, which he hated.

One of Dickens' novels, *Oliver Twist*, is about an orphan who is badly treated in a workhouse.

Workhouse masters

Some workhouse masters were cruel, but many did their best to look after the poor in their care. What impression of workhouses do you get from the photograph and diary entries on page 19?

Watch a film

Charles Dickens' story of *Oliver Twist* has been made into a film. Borrow a copy to find out what happened to him.

A well-known part of Dickens' novel is where Oliver Twist asks for more gruel.

Dec 1837

The inmates had all plenty of Roast Beef and Plum Pudding on Christmas Day and was very comfortable except the Cook who got intoxicated soon after dinner. We sent her to bed.

Mar 1838

Elizabeth Signell, aged 46, and her 7 children was admitted in the house by order of Removal and Relieving Officer on Wednesday 6 March. Paupers of South Mimms, George aged 13, Elizabeth 11, Mary 7, Diana 5 and the Mother stopped. The other 3 went back to London all having situations to go to. They were in a most wretched condition, naked and starved.

Mar 1838

William Marlborough aged 18, pauper of Ridge, wishes to go out on Friday, if the Board will provide him with some clothing. He was admitted on 15 February so filthy dirty we was obliged to burn all his rags.

April 1838

The Rev Mr Thackery sent a quantity of Toys and Dolls to the Workhouse on Saturday for the use of the Boys and Girls.

These are entries from a diary kept by Benjamin Woodcock, the Master of Barnet Workhouse. What impressions does he give you?

These children at Hitchin workhouse, in about 1880, are all wearing the same clothes. This was the workhouse uniform and meant that everyone knew they were paupers.

Help for street children

In 1881 two brothers were found begging for food in London. Their father had died, leaving their mother with seven children. She did not want the family to go into a workhouse, so the boys had to fend for themselves. The man who found them was so concerned that he founded the Waifs and Strays Society to help homeless and hungry children.

Other people were concerned about children sleeping on the streets, especially in towns. Dr Barnardo (1845-1905) opened a shelter for destitute boys in London. These children also found help at the Ragged Schools.

Crime and punishment

Homeless or hungry children could easily get into trouble with the law. In early Victorian times, these children were treated in the same way as adults. They could be put into adult prisons alongside hardened criminals.

Many crimes had the death penalty. A child aged 10 could be hanged for arson or for stealing a sheep.

Name	Thomas Groves
Colour of hair	Dark brown
Complexion	Pale
Eyes	Hazel
Marks (if any)	2 scars on right side of face. Scar on back of neck. Scar inside right leg.
Age	13
Married or single	Single
Read or write	Imperfect
Trade or profession	Labourer
When and where convicted	2 January 1845, Maidstone Sessions
Description of crime	Stealing wearing apparel
Sentence	7 years
Information received respecting prisoner	Is supposed to have lived in crime about 5 years. Once imprisoned for having lodged in an outhouse. Was left when an infant at the door of a house in Whitechapel.
Imprisoned: when and where	2 January 1845, Maidstone Gaol; 17 January 1845, Millbank Prison; 25 February 1845, Parkhurst Prison
Discharged: when and where	3 August 1849, Van Dieman's Land

▼ *Use this information from Parkhurst prison register to find out what crimes Thomas Groves had committed. How do you think his life would be different if he was born today?*

▼ *George Davey, aged 10, was imprisoned for one month with hard labour in Wandsworth Gaol for stealing two tame rabbits. Why do you think he might have done this?*

Transported across the sea

An alternative to the death penalty was transportation. The person was sent to another country. Thomas Groves was transported to Van Dieman's Land for seven years. This is an island south of Australia, now called Tasmania. The ship that carried Thomas and other prisoners took three months to get there.

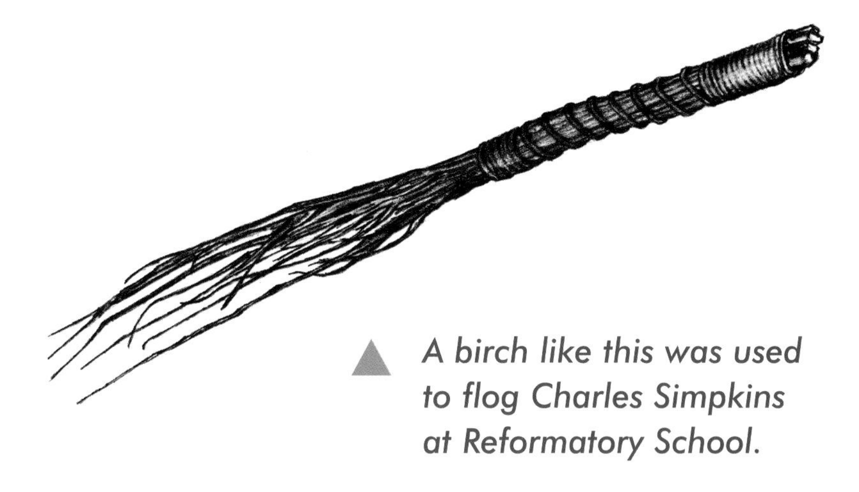

▲ *A birch like this was used to flog Charles Simpkins at Reformatory School.*

Changes for the better

During Queen Victoria's reign several changes made things better for children accused or found guilty of crimes.

- From 1847 children accused of crimes were tried in children's courts.
- In 1854 Reformatory Schools were set up to try to give children a new start by removing them from bad influences.
- In 1868 transportation was ended.
- Finally, from 1899, children were no longer sent to adult prisons.

Reformatory Schools

Children were often sentenced to several years at a Reformatory School and had to go to adult prison first. For stealing some money, Charles Simpkins, aged 11, was sentenced to 21 days in prison and 2 years in Reformatory School. The School Admission Register records Charles's behaviour at the school. At first he got into trouble for 'very untidy habits' and was beaten six times with 'the birch' for stealing grapes from the garden. But in 1873, after Charles had left the school and got a job, his Master wrote a letter saying 'he is doing well'. Do you think the Reformatory School helped him to change?

Hold a discussion

What do you think about corporal punishment (beating or smacking)? The Victorians thought it was good for children. Does punishment help stop crime? Is it more important to punish someone who behaves badly, or to try to change how they behave in future?

Free schools for all

How could you stop children getting into trouble? The Victorians believed that children needed to be taught rules for how to behave. For this, they needed to go to school. The problem was that there were not enough schools. At the beginning of Queen Victoria's reign, half of all children could not read or write.

What choices did people have?

For rich families there were boarding schools for the boys, and a governess at home for the girls. Middle-class children went to private schools. In towns, there were charity schools or Ragged Schools for the very poor.

Church schools, called National and British Schools, provided a basic education for working-class children. They had to pay a weekly amount, known as 'school pence'.

These were the rules for the National Schools in Paddington, London. They show how important good behaviour – 'morals, manners and conduct' – was, at home as well as at school. What is different and what is the same, compared with your school rules?

RULES

TO BE OBSERVED BY THE PARENTS AND CHILDREN

I. Parents are required to pay Two Pence weekly to the Master or Mistress on Monday morning, in advance, for their first and second Child, and One Penny each for every other Child whom they may send to the School.

II. All Scholars must appear at the School punctually at Nine in the Morning, and Two in the Afternoon, with their hands and faces clean, their hair cut and combed, and their clothes neatly mended.

III. No Child is permitted to stay at home without leave from the Master or Mistress, except in case of illness, of which immediate notice must be given either in person or in writing.

IV. No Child who does not attend regularly, will be permitted to stay in the School.

V. It is earnestly desired that Parents will take all possible care of their Children's morals, manners and conduct, before and after the hours of School, and will not allow them to be running about in the Evening after it is dark, or be playing about on Sundays.

"Train up a Child in the way he should go, and when he is old he will not depart from it."

Education Acts

William Forster was unhappy that not every child had the chance to go to school. In 1870 he persuaded Parliament to pass an Education Act setting up state schools where there were not enough church schools. These new schools, called Board Schools, were really three schools in one: an infants' school for boys and girls between 3 and 7 years old and separate schools for boys and girls aged 7 to 13. Now there were schools for everyone. However, children did not have to go to school until 1880, when another Education Act made school compulsory for children under 10. Finally, in 1891, school fees were abolished, and education became free for all children aged 5 to 13.

Here is a class at Boxmoor School, about 1900. On the right is Dora Spice. She was a pupil teacher, in charge of the class from the age of 13. Pupil teachers did their own lessons before school in the morning, and in the evening. In 1905 Dora went to college to become a qualified teacher.

History detective

Go to your local library and ask for books about your local area. Look for photographs of children at school in Victorian times. You might even find pictures of your own school.

In the classroom

Classes were very big. One teacher could have as many as 90 children. The infants were often looked after by monitors, girls aged 10 to 12. Monitors could go on to be pupil teachers.

What did they learn?

Reading, writing and arithmetic were the most important subjects. They were known as 'the three Rs'. There were also 'Moral Lessons'.

What differences are there between St Marylebone Charity School for Girls in 1890 and your classroom today? The girls are writing on slates. They are wearing smocks or pinafores to keep their dresses clean.

General Gordon slain at Khartoum, 1885.
General Gordon slain at Khartoum, 1885.
General Gordon slain at Khartoum, 1885.
General Gordon slain at Khartoum, 1885.
Burmah annexed to Great Britain, 1886.
Burmah annexed to Great Britain, 1886.
Burmah annexed to Great Britain, 1886.
Burmah annexed to Great Britain, 1886.

To practise writing, children used a copybook. They had to copy a printed sentence several times on the lines underneath. Their copies had to look exactly the same. Can you copy these sentences exactly? Victorian children wrote with a steel-nibbed pen dipped in ink.

This extract is from the logbook of Whiteshill National School. Would Rev. Anstey have approved of a Moral Lesson taught at Two Waters School on 'Idleness ... Its curse, How prevented'?

For exercise, children did 'drill' in the playground, following the teacher's orders to march up and down, bend and stretch.

Drill practice

Imagine you are teaching drill in a Victorian school. Work out a routine you could shout orders for. Try it out with your friends.

1879. Jan 11th

An unusually severe week which has greatly affected the attendance of the children... On Wednesday afternoon, the number of children being very low, and the school extremely cold, the master collected them into one class, and read to them a story of North American life, from a quarter past two till three o'clock.

The Rev A. C. C. Anstey came in during the reading, and found fault with the arrangement, and on Friday Morning brought a letter to the master on the subject of which the following is a copy:

Whiteshill Vicarage,
Stroud
Jan 10. 1879.

Dear Mr Cull,

For many reasons I am very sorry to have to make any complaints about the school, but as a manager I think it my duty not to pass without notice my coming into the school on Wednesday afternoon and finding you reading a story book to the children during the regular school hours.

Whatever may be said about the small attendance, I can only regard it as a very serious irregularity at the least, and hope it may never occur again under any circumstances.

Of course I could not speak my real opinion in front of the children, and indeed it appeared to me such a startling thing that I have taken time to consider what I ought to do. Whether one considers the parents of the children, the example to the young pupil teachers, or the requirements of the government, I can only regret very much that such a thing should go on in the school at any time whatever.

Yours truly
(Signed) A. C. C. Anstey

What changed for poor children?

Life changed much more for poor children than for rich ones between 1837 and 1901. Rich children had always been able to go to school, and not have to work. For poor children, life became much better. They could all go to school, and should not have to work before they were 12. Perhaps life for children in the country changed less than for children in the towns. School logbooks show that many children were still kept away from school to work on farms, at least at certain times of year.

> The average attendance this week is much reduced by a number of boys being imployed in harvest work, & others being required to take the necessary meals to their fathers &c.

This is a logbook entry for August 1871, from a school at Watton-at-Stone. Why were some children absent?

The Ten Hours Act (1847) limited the number of hours children worked in factories, but some children still worked long hours at home. This family in Bethnal Green in 1900 are making brushes. Can you see who has fallen asleep?

Attitudes to children

The most important change was in the way people thought about children. In 1837 children were treated at work and by the law as the same as adults. In 1901 people thought that childhood was a special time and children should be treated differently.

By the end of Victorian times children had more leisure time, like these playing in a Luton park in 1900.

Early Victorians thought children were naturally bad, and needed the badness beaten out of them. Charles Dickens helped to change people's minds through the characters in his novels. In *David Copperfield*, his villains are the Murdstones who believe that all children are 'a swarm of little vipers'. The hero is little David, a good child unfairly treated.

The effect on our lives

Look back through this book and make a list of changes that happened. Use two columns: one for bad practices that stopped, and one for good practices that started. Which of these changes has had most effect on your life today?

Proverbs

An early Victorian proverb: 'Spare the rod and spoil the child.'

A late Victorian proverb: 'All work and no play makes Jack a dull boy.'

Try making up a new proverb about children today.

Glossary

Act law passed by Parliament.

arson setting fire to a building or someone's property.

bank holidays special days, first given in 1871, when banks and other workplaces are closed so that everyone has a holiday.

birch bundle of twigs used to beat children.

blacking black paste or shoe polish.

Board Schools schools set up by Forster's Education Act (1870), run by locally elected Boards of Governors.

bobbins cylinders or cones holding thread in machines used to weave cloth.

British Schools schools set up by churches other than the Church of England, such as Methodists and Baptists, through the British and Foreign Schools Society (founded in 1814).

census information about everyone who lives in England and Wales, collected every 10 years from 1801 onwards (with names from 1841). The returns can be seen after 100 years.

charity schools schools set up from the end of the seventeenth century with money given to help meet the needs of the poor.

Commission of Enquiry group of people asked by Parliament to find out about a particular issue by visiting places and interviewing witnesses.

copybook book containing good examples of handwriting for learners to copy.

coroner officer of a court holding inquests (inquiries) into violent or accidental deaths.

d (e.g. 3d) old pence, the currency used in Britain up until 1971.

death penalty punishment by being put to death.

deformed not the shape it should be.

degraded made to feel bad because you have to do something wrong or unworthy of you.

destitute without food or shelter.

drill exercise by obeying commands and following a strict routine, like the military drill performed by soldiers.

exploited taken advantage of by others for their own ends.

governess woman employed to teach children at home.

hard labour heavy manual work as a punishment in prison.

hurriers girls (or sometimes boys) who pulled trucks loaded with coal in coalmines.

inquest inquiry into the cause of a death.

logbooks daily records kept by headteachers, including information about school attendance and lessons taught.

mine shaft hole in the ground, usually hundreds of feet deep, connecting the surface to the underground tunnels in a mine.

monitors older children at school who spent some of their time teaching younger groups of children.

moral lessons lessons to learn the difference between right and wrong.

mourning period (usually no more than a year) after someone died when people wore black to show their sadness.

MP Member of Parliament, elected to represent the views of the people and make laws for the country.

National Schools schools set up by the Church of England's National Society for the Education of the Poor (founded 1811).

oppressed harshly or cruelly treated.

oral history spoken memories of the past.

orphan child whose parents have died.

overlooker person in a mill or factory responsible for making sure children worked hard.

pauper destitute person supported by charity.

propaganda spreading a message in a way that may be misleading or dishonest.

pupil teacher pupil aged 13 or over who taught a class, received a small salary and after five years could go on to college to become a fully qualified teacher.

Ragged Schools inner-city schools for the poorest children who had no shoes and only tattered clothes to wear.

Reformatory Schools schools set up in 1854 to improve the behaviour of children who had been in prison.

reminiscence remembering the past and writing it down or telling someone about it.

respectable polite or proper in behaviour.

scavengers small children who had to gather the loose threads and cotton waste that collected on the floor under big machines in textile mills.

sentence time spent in prison or a Reformatory School as a punishment.

slate smooth, flat piece of grey rock framed in wood for writing on with a slate pencil (a small rod of soft slate) and cleaned with a sponge.

state schools schools set up by the government.

textile mills buildings with machines for making cloth, such as cotton, silk or wool.

transportation removal by ship to another country, as a punishment.

trappers children in coalmines who had to open doors in underground tunnels for coal trucks to pass through.

typhoid disease caused by contaminated water, leading to a high fever and often death.

Victorians people who lived during the reign of Queen Victoria, 1837-1901.

waifs and strays abandoned children.

workhouse place where orphans, the poor, sick and disabled were housed and put to work. Conditions were horrible to discourage people from seeking help unless they were really desperate.

For teachers and parents

Looking at the lives of children in Victorian Britain, we realise how much of what we take for granted, such as going to school and time to play, was achieved so recently. Campaigners like Lord Shaftesbury worked tirelessly to improve life for children. Remembering their efforts can inspire us to tackle exploitation and injustice in our world today.

Changing attitudes to childhood during Victorian times gave rise to a key source of information on children's working lives. The reports of the various Commissions of Enquiry published during the 19th century cover the whole of England and Wales. The Minutes of Evidence in the Appendices to these reports contain transcripts of interviews with children which give us detailed and often moving, firsthand accounts.

A wealth of documentary evidence shows us children at home, at school, in prisons and workhouses. Interpreting the evidence poses a considerable challenge. Much was produced by campaigners seeking social justice. Whether it is the novels of Charles Dickens or pictures in the *Illustrated London News*, we need to ask how the author's intention might affect the message. Even photographs can be misleading: many showing destitute children were carefully posed for the purpose of fund raising. The reliability of oral evidence also needs to be questioned.

Exploring life in Victorian Britain gives children an unparalleled opportunity to engage with a wide range of sources. In using these sources in their historical enquiry, the children can be encouraged to question the evidence, compare different ways in which the past is represented, and express their own ideas.

There are opportunities for cross-curricular work, particularly in literacy, mathematics, geography, science, religious education and citizenship. ICT plays an important part in supporting children's learning as they work through the book.

SUGGESTED FURTHER ACTIVITIES

Pages 4 – 5 Queen Victoria
To develop a sense of chronology, you could do some more work around family trees. Talk about relationships. What relationship is Queen Victoria to Prince William? You could add Prince Harry to this family tree. Children could draw their own family trees.

Get a copy of a Victorian census (e.g. 1851) for your local area. Use several pages so the children can do a survey to find the most popular children's names. Compare this with a survey of names in the class. Are any the same? Present the results in the form of bar charts.

Pages 6 – 7 Family fun
Children could make their own thaumatrope, a popular Victorian toy. You can download a template from the website of the Museum of Childhood: www.vam.ac.uk/moc/things_to_make/thaumatrope/index.html.

Pages 8 – 9 Life on the land
You could use the picture of the young bird scarer as a stimulus for creative writing. Alternatively, children could imagine they are the bird scarer as an old man, giving their 'personal reminiscence'.

Research Victorian homes and see if you can find out how many rooms Thomas Hole's cottage might have had.

School logbooks often mention children in rural areas being absent for haymaking, gleaning, potato picking and even acorn gathering. If your school logbooks have not survived, contact your nearest Archives or Record Office to see logbooks for other schools in the area.

Pages 10 – 11 Factories
The top picture on page 11 was drawn in 1835 for a book celebrating the progress of the cotton industry in Britain. The picture at the bottom left is from Frances Trollope's book, *Michael Armstrong: Factory Boy* (1840). This used the same picture but added and altered details to convey a very different message. The centre picture, a cartoon from the 1840s, is a piece of popular propaganda. Although sensationalist, it does highlight the inhumane conditions that were operating in some (but not all) factories. You might ask the children to: (1) Compare the top and bottom pictures. (2) Have a caption competition. (3) Look at adverts in magazines to find examples of pictures that may mislead.

Pages 12 – 13 Mines
Children could use ICT to present the causes of death in a form other than a table: e.g. graph, bar chart, pie chart. Convert the numbers into percentages. Discuss how (a) a mine owner and (b) a campaigner for children's rights might choose to present the information.

Research the reason for gas explosions in coalmines. Children could find out about the Davy Safety Lamp and how it worked.

Pages 14 – 15 Chimney-sweeps
Mrs Mary Dye took over the chimney-sweep business after her husband's death. If she told the story to her grandchildren, it might explain why Daniel Dye told it through her eyes. (He told the story to a journalist in 1952.) Use the two accounts to introduce children to the difference between primary and secondary sources. To extend this work you could ask children to: (1) Make a list of primary sources (those recorded at the time). (2) Make a list of secondary sources (distanced

by time or by place). (3) List advantages and disadvantages of primary and secondary sources as evidence. (4) Play Chinese Whispers to show how a story can change over time.

Role-play the inquest into the death of James Dye, with the coroner as the judge cross-examining witnesses. The rest of the class are the jury.

Pages 16 – 17 Lord Shaftesbury
To develop skills in using pictures as evidence, take a closer look at the picture of Lord Shaftesbury visiting the Ragged School. (1) Who is shown in the picture? (2) Why might it have been painted? (3) Who might it have been for? (4) How accurate is it likely to be? The painting has a feel-good factor. The children look clean and well fed. It is not designed to shock but would make the philanthropists in the picture feel important, and perhaps encourage others to give to a good cause.

You could find out more about Adeline Cooper, the 'Heroine of the Devil's Acre'. An album of her letters, including a letter written by one of the One Tun Ragged School pupils, and a letter from Lord Shaftesbury to the children, can be seen at Westminster City Archives.

Pages 18 – 19 Life in the workhouse
What questions would you like to ask Charles Dickens about his world? Ask the children what they would ask him. Can they think what his answers might be?

Send an e-card with a picture of Victorian children to a friend. See: www.hiddenlives.org.uk.

Pages 20 – 21 Crime and punishment
Use an atlas to find Tasmania, and work out how many miles Thomas Groves travelled. The children could draw a map of his journey and plot the route that his ship might have taken.

Imagine the class has landed on a deserted island. Ask each child to draw up a set of laws for their new country. Then make a poster telling people what punishments will be given if they break these laws.

How will the class agree on which laws and punishments they will use? Create a mock Parliament to discuss the issues and reach a decision.

If possible, arrange a visit to your local magistrates court.

Pages 22 – 23 Free schools for all
Ask the children to find out about the history of your school. What can they find out from looking at the building? Are there any school buildings in your community which are now used for something else? See if you can find a National School or a Board School in your area. Take photographs of any you find and mount a display.

Ask children to copy and paste the timetable of a workhouse school in the 1840s from www.workhouses.org. Convert the timetable into a table with three columns: (1) the hours of the day; (2) the Victorian school timetable; (3) their own timetable for a chosen day.

Pages 24 – 25 In the classroom
A Victorian school logbook listed the following subjects for 'Moral Lessons': Honesty, Truthfulness, Obedience, Order, Love for Home, Industry, Kindness, Cruelty, Punctuality, Love for School, Idleness, Patience, Perseverance, Gratitude, Cheerfulness, Cleanliness, Forgiveness. Write each of these on a card and make enough sets for the children to work in groups. Let them sort the cards into words they know the meaning of and those they don't. Use dictionaries to find the meanings and write definitions. You could also play 'Just a Minute': volunteers pick a card out of a hat and see how long they can talk about the subject without stopping.

Pages 26 – 27 What changed for poor children?
Dates and events could be written on separate cards and a game played to match dates with events and then sequence them.

1837	Queen Victoria comes to the throne.
1838	Charles Dickens publishes *Oliver Twist*.
1840	Chimney Sweep Act tries to stop children being sent up chimneys (but they still are).
1842	Mines Act stops children under 10 working in coalmines.
1844	Lord Shaftesbury becomes president of Ragged School Union
1846	Pupil teacher system begins.
1847	Ten Hours Act stops children aged 13-18 working more than 10 hours a day in factories
1854	Reformatory Schools set up.
1860	Mines Act stops children under 12 working in coalmines.
1861	Prince Albert dies of typhoid.
1870	Forster's Education Act sets up schools for all children aged 5–10 (but they still have to pay).
1873	Agricultural Act stops children under 8 working on farms.
1875	Lord Shaftesbury's Chimney Sweeps Act stops children being sent up chimneys (this time it succeeds).
1880	School is compulsory for all children aged 5-10.
1891	Free education for all children aged 5-13.
1901	Queen Victoria dies and her son becomes King Edward VII.

ADDITIONAL RESOURCES

Reports of Commissions of Enquiry can be found in university libraries and large reference libraries. Archive CD Books has produced a facsimile copy of evidence given to the Children's Employment Commission (1842) on CD-Rom. Primary sources can be found at your local archives, record office or local studies library. For contact details see www.nationalarchives.gov.uk.

The National Archives have an excellent education section at http://nationalarchives.gov.uk/education/.

'Gathering the Jewels' contains thousands of documents, photographs and objects held by archives, libraries and museums across Wales. www.gtj.org.uk/en/

Index